GRAN CANARIA TRAVEL GUIDE 2024

Your Insider's Compass to the Island's Wonders:
Beaches, Hikes, and Hidden Gems

Judith R. Rivera

Table of Contents

1. INTRODUCTION TO GRAN CANARIA

A: Welcome to the Island's Wonders

The volcanic island of Gran Canaria is a treasure in the Atlantic Ocean. Gran Canaria, one of the seven Canary Islands, is a culturally and topographically diverse melting pot of peoples and ways of life. This amazing island, which is often called a "continent in miniature," has the finest climate in the world, with sunlight and warmth all year round thanks to its eternal spring.

Gran Canaria welcomes sightseers with a surreal medley of mountainous landscapes, arid plains, lush woods, and cliff-lined coastlines—all in a comparatively small area. Exploring the island's many hidden gems will reveal a wealth of sights and sounds, from the majestic Maspalomas dunes—like a tiny Sahara—to the ancient Vegueta lanes in Las Palmas, the main city.

Upon reaching the island, one can smell the salt in the air and hear the melodies of a language that has been influenced by both Spanish and indigenous Guanche influences. Colorful building facades, traditional music with exuberant rhythms, and friendly locals all contribute to the island's lively spirit.

As the traveler makes their way down the twisting roads, a completely unexpected environment, complete with fresh scenes and climates, unfolds before them. Explorers may travel to the heights of Pico de las Nieves, the island's highest mountain, to watch the sky pink at sunset, or delve into the deep of the old laurel woods in Los Tilos de Moya, a green throwback to the Tertiary era.

And then there are the beaches—over 60 kilometers of them—ranging from the crowded coastlines full of laughter and play to isolated coves where the waves whisper secrets to the sands. It's an island that offers adventure for the thrill-seeker, relaxation for the sun-worshiper, and enlightenment for the culture-enthused.

The island of Gran Canaria is known for its lively festivals, with fiestas happening daily. Each village and neighborhood has its distinct style of rejoicing, from the bright Carnival of Las Palmas to the serious rites of Semana Santa. The cuisine is a fiesta in its own right, with a spread that brings the wealth of the sea to the table, mixed with tastes and skills passed down through generations.

As you commence on the voyage throughout this wonderful isle, every road leads to a discovery, from the craggy northern shores to the placid southern beaches, from the quiet villages to the busy metropolitan areas. Gran Canaria encourages you to enjoy its delights, revel in what the island freely provides, and carry out memories on its beaches that will call you to return.

In this island where every particle of sand has a tale, where each wave sings a ballad of the centuries, and where the mountains stand as guardians of millennia—Gran Canaria doesn't simply welcome you, it captivates your spirit. And so starts your voyage on this island of miracles.

B: What Makes Gran Canaria a Unique Destination

Gran Canaria, a treasure inside the Canary Islands, is an exquisite place that expands like a little continent. There's a patchwork of varied temperatures and spectacular scenery, which span from the lush woods of the north to the sun-baked southern dunes that seem to whisper stories of the Sahara.

This Spanish island is unusual, not simply in its landscape, but in its capacity to deliver a microcosm of experiences. The cultural diversity of Gran Canaria is palpable—from its indigenous pre-Hispanic origins, seen in the cave dwellings and ancient murals of Cuevas Pintadas, to its colonial past shown in the cobblestone lanes of Vegueta in the capital city, Las Palmas.

Gran Canaria's distinctiveness also radiates from its beaches. Playa de Maspalomas is a highlight with its changing dunes designated as a nature reserve. Here, nature constructs an ever-changing vista, while the adjacent Playa del Inglés is a frenetic length catering to visitors seeking exciting beachfront and exuberant nightlife.

The island's heart, however, beats in its rough core. Roque Nublo and Pico de las

Nieves provide not only hiking trails but also vantage places where the island's beauty spreads in an unending perspective. The pine-clad mountains produce not only scenic splendors but also ecological richness sustaining a variety of flora and wildlife. The Laurisilva woods in the north bear the remains of the Tertiary era, affording a look into prehistoric times.

The climate of Gran Canaria is commonly characterized as an 'eternal spring'. This phenomenon is attributed to the trade winds and the Canary Current, which offer the isla steady and pleasant weather year-round. It's a shelter for individuals leaving colder areas, providing the promise of sunlight even in the depths of winter.

Gran Canaria is not simply ecosystems and geography—it's also a cultural crossroads. Festivals like the yearly Carnival bring the island to life with a kaleidoscope of colors and costumes, reminiscent of Rio de

Janeiro's exuberant energy. Artisan markets, indigenous crafts, and a gastronomic adventure that covers the ocean's richness and Spanish culinary traditions increase the island's charm.

The gastronomy is a mix of its rich history and agricultural richness. Tropical fruits grow in abundance, fresh seafood is a mainstay, and local specialties such as "papas arrugadas" (wrinkled potatoes) with a hot "mojo" sauce tempt guests to revel in native tastes.

In terms of sustainability, Gran Canaria has made progress in maintaining its beauty for future generations. Efforts in renewable energy, water desalination, and maintaining natural ecosystems guarantee that tourism stays responsible and appreciative of this unique environment.

For the tourist seeking a combination of adventure, leisure, and cultural discovery,

Gran Canaria is a treasure trove. A year-round mild temperature, diversified landscapes, rich history, and inviting local ambiance make the island an unparalleled location for visitors wishing to enjoy a bit of everything within a small and accessible region. Gran Canaria stands as an embodiment of nature's generosity, and human history, and a celebration of life's delights all on one island—a truly unique location.

2. GETTING ACQUAINTED WITH GRAN CANARIA

A: Overview of the Island's Geography and Climate

In the Canaries, an archipelago off the northwest coast of Africa that is a part of Spain, Gran Canaria is the third-largest island. Because of its varied terrain, which varies from lush forests in the north to deserts in the south, and steep mountains in the middle, this subtropical island is sometimes referred to as a "continent in miniature".

The island is geographically formed like a circle, with a circumference of around thirty-one miles, or fifty kilometers. With a height of 1,949 meters (6,394 feet), the tallest mountain in the area, Pico de las

Nieves, dominates the scene. This island's central highland is a portion of the Cumbre, a hilly region that forms the island's spine and radiates downhill into deep valleys and gorges. For an island of small, these features combine to create microclimates that vary significantly over short distances.

Gran Canaria has a year-round moderate and pleasant climate, which has given the Canary Islands the moniker "Islands of Eternal Spring." The average yearly temperature on the island is around 24°C (75°F), however, local conditions and altitude might affect this. Because of the mountains that protect it from the trade winds, the south of the island often experiences milder temperatures and more sunlight. The northeastern winds provide moisture and colder air to the island's northern regions, resulting in a greener and more moderate environment.

The intriguing phenomenon known as "Panza de burro" (donkey belly), which is caused by the combination of the trade winds and the chilly Canary Current, is when a layer of low-lying clouds may linger over the northeast of the island even while the southern regions are bathed in sunlight.

Rainfall is scarce, particularly in the island's south, which is often dryer. Rainfall occurs mostly in the winter months of November through February, with the possibility of larger downpours in hilly locations, which contributes to the preservation of vegetation in such places. On the other hand, due to its dry environment, the southern portion of the island is popular with visitors looking for sun and sand since it has large dunes and beaches, such as those at Maspalomas.

Gran Canaria is a special place because of its climate and terrain. This island provides a variety of settings to appreciate, whether one is interested in trekking through deep pine woods, exploring desert regions, or just relaxing on golden beaches. The island's culture and way of life are also shaped by this variety, adjusting to a place where a few kilometers may bring drastic weather changes.

B: Historical and Cultural Importance

Situated in the Atlantic Ocean, Gran Canaria is a subtropical island and the third biggest of the Canary Islands archipelago belonging to Spain. It's important geographic location, European colonization, and indigenous ancestry all contribute to its cultural and historical value.

Original Origins:
The Guanches, the island's first residents, are said to have descended from Berbers in North Africa. Their roots are the starting point of the narrative of Gran Canaria.

These people had a complex social structure, extensive cultural traditions, and varied living arrangements, ranging from communal towns to cave homes. Many of these customs were centered on the natural world and their agricultural way of life. The cryptic symbols of this ancient and mostly unknown society are still cave paintings and petroglyphs.

The Arrival and Colonization of Europeans:
The island's historical turning point occurred when European expansionism focused on it in the fifteenth century. Gran Canaria fell to the Castilians in 1483 after a long struggle that ended the Guanche way of life. Gran Canaria was an important location in the Spanish Empire and became a crossroads for European journeys to the Americas and Africa after Spanish annexation.

Cultural Fusion Center:

The island's capital, Las Palmas, was a crucial stopping point in the Atlantic due to its large port, which throughout the ages brought together Europeans, Africans, and Americans. This blended with the remnants of Guanche culture to create the customs and traditions that still exist on the island today.

Festivities and Religious Influence:
The Spanish introduced Catholicism, which left its mark on the local way of life via imposing cathedrals and holy celebrations. The Fiesta de San Juan and the Feast of Our Lady of the Pine, which combine local traditions with Catholic traditions in lively festivities, are two examples of the island's religious devotion.

History of Architecture:
Ancient communal granaries known as the Cenobio de Valerón and elegant colonial buildings like the Casa de Colón in Las Palmas, which capture the island's

significance in Christopher Columbus's voyages to the Americas, are just two examples of the island's striking historical architectural influences.

Changes in the Economy:
Agriculture has always been the main source of income on the island, with sugar cane and subsequently bananas serving as cash crops. With the island's good temperature, varied scenery, and rich history, the tourist sector flourished in the 20th century and became a major economic force.

Historical Heritage:
The rich past of Gran Canaria is reflected in the island's current culture. Folk music and canarian wrestling, or lucha canaria, are combined with contemporary cuisine that combines native ingredients with Spanish and Latin American influences. Internationally renowned festivals such as the Carnival of Las Palmas include a vivid assortment of dances, costumes, and music

that reflect the island's multifarious cultural heritage.

Changes and influences have shaped Gran Canaria's history from the Guanche to the present, culminating in a unique cultural identity. Its strategic location has given it historical importance on a worldwide scale, and the island's current cultural environment is nevertheless shaped by the enduring effects of its colonial and indigenous past.

3. EXPLORING THE BEACHES OF GRAN CANARIA

A: Tour of the Most Gorgeous Beaches on the Island

Known for its variety of scenery, from the lush and verdant north to the arid south, Gran Canaria, one of the Canary Islands, is a brilliant gem in the Atlantic Ocean. The beaches on this little continent are its greatest assets. Here, we'll start our exploration of some of Gran Canaria's most breathtaking beaches.

Maspalomas Beach

The well-known Playa de Maspalomas, located at the southernmost point of the island, is well-known for its extensive dune system, which has been designated as a natural reserve. This beach has golden sands that flow seamlessly into Playa del Inglés for around 6 kilometers. It's a true paradise by the sea. The dunes provide a feeling of being in a desert and are a breathtaking sight at dusk. Families like the eastern end because of the calmer seas; this end is closest to the Maspalomas lighthouse.

Las Canteras Beach

Playa de Las Canteras, the vibrant urban beach in Las Palmas' capital, is well-known for its busy promenade and the "barra," a naturally occurring rock structure that protects a portion of the beach from waves. Stretching around 2.5 kilometers, it's a cultural melting pot with plenty of room for surfing, snorkeling, and swimming. The shoreline is a social center as well since it is dotted with eateries and shops.

Playa de Mogán

Also known as "Little Venice," Puerto de Mogán is a quaint little beach. The town's canals, which are the area's main feature, are what gave rise to the moniker. Swimming is safe here because of the calm waters provided by the protected harbor. The beach is part of a charming, picturesque port that is teeming with vibrant structures and plenty of waterfront restaurants.

The Amadores Beach

Playa de Amadores is a cove beach and man-made wonder, renowned for its calm, turquoise seas and white sand imported from the Caribbean. With craggy rocks all around, it seems remote. The beach is well-equipped with features including umbrellas, sun loungers, and many restaurants with sea views. It's the ideal location for a laid-back family trip.

Puerto Rico's Playa

Playa de Puerto Rico, which is located in one of Gran Canaria's sunniest spots, offers recreational opportunities. Water activities including windsurfing, sailing, and jet skiing gather along the beach. This beach has calm waves, good sand, and a bustling promenade with a wide selection of eateries and stores.

Güi Güi Beach

Rugged and remote Playa de Güi Güi is a must-see for adventure seekers. This beach's appeal and unspoiled beauty are increased by the fact that it can only be reached by boat or a strenuous climb. With its black volcanic sand and charming seclusion, it offers a natural haven away from the more populated beaches.

The Alcaravaneras Beach

Another hidden treasure in Las Palmas is Playa de las Alcaravaneras, a famous local beach with golden sand that receives relatively little visitor traffic. With one of the city's marinas on one side and a background of yachts and boats on the other, it's a great place for activities like beach volleyball and kayaking.

Every beach on Gran Canaria has its distinct charm and array of activities, telling a distinctive tale. Gran Canaria's coastline provides a little piece of heaven for every beach lover, whether they choose peaceful, natural getaways or a busy beachfront with all the facilities necessary. You may write a fascinating travelog chapter about your time spent on these sandy coastlines.

B: Water Activities and Leisure by the Beach

Glistening like a gem in the Atlantic, Gran Canaria provides an amazing surface for a wide variety of water activities in addition to its serene beaches for leisure.

Gran Canaria Water Sports

The island is a haven for lovers of water sports due to its diverse shoreline and consistent winds. Here's a sampling of what's available:

Surfing:
Waves to suit all skill levels can be found along the northern coast at beaches like Las Canteras and El Confital. For beginners, there are plenty of surf schools and rentals available, while more experienced surfers

like to chase the waves in more remote locations.

Kitesurfing and Windsurfing:
International contests are held at Pozo Izquierdo, an east coast town known for its powerful winds. Additionally, Vargas Beach and Playa de Sotavento provide great conditions for novices and experts alike.

Scuba Diving and Snorkeling:
Underwater exploration is a paradise in Gran Canaria's crystal-clear seas. Rich marine biodiversity may be found at Arinaga's El Cabrón Marine Reserve, and interesting diving spots can be found close to Tufia thanks to man made reefs. Snorkelers may enjoy Las Canteras' natural aquarium or Playa de Amadores' tranquil seas.

Jet Skiing and Parasailing:
Rentable jet skis are available in popular locations like Puerto Rico and Anfi del Mar,

and they provide an exhilarating rush for thrill-seekers. Another well-liked pastime is parasailing, which provides amazing aerial views of the island's topography.

Sailing and Boat trips:
There are many possibilities to see dolphins and whales on sailing and catamaran trips, which allow you to enjoy the island's natural beauty from the ocean.

Canoeing and Stand-up Paddleboarding (SUP):
SUP and canoeing aficionados find the ideal conditions in the mild southern waves, especially at Morgan and Playa de Molino de Viento.

Soothness along the Shore

Gran Canaria does not let down people looking for peace:

Playa de Maspalomas and Playa del Inglés:

Fronted by gorgeous dunes, these well-known beaches provide plenty of room for leisure.

Playa de Amadores:
Its white sand is wonderful for sunbathing, and its protected harbor and calm seas make it the perfect place for tranquil swimming.

Las Canteras:
After a day by the sea, relax in one of the many cafés and restaurants along the lively promenade.

Montaña de Arena:
With its golden beaches and a comparatively off-the-beaten-path vibe, this is a more sedate choice for leisure.

Wellness Resorts:
A lot of resorts and spas make use of the peaceful beach environment to provide relaxation treatments, such as thalassotherapy (using saltwater).

Beachfront Yoga:
Several places offer group classes, and the tranquility of Gran Canaria's mornings makes it ideal for yoga by the sea.

Gran Canaria creates a special environment where adventure and calm coexist together by fusing the energy of water activities with coastlines that whisper quiet. The island welcomes everyone who comes to its beaches, whether they are seeking the surf or the serene sunsets.

4. EXPLORING GRAN CANARIA'S NATURAL BEAUTY

A: Hiking Trails and Nature Reserves

Beyond its beaches, Gran Canaria has an abundance of hiking paths and environmental reserves that highlight the island's diverse topography and ecosystem. Discovering the island's inner areas will allow you to properly appreciate its rich biodiversity and distinctive microclimates.

Natural Areas and Pathways for Hiking

Tejeda Caldera and Roque Nublo:
The striking rock Roque Nublo, regarded as the island's natural icon, dominates Central Gran Canaria. There are several routes in the vicinity of Tejeda Caldera, one of which

goes to the foot of Roque Nublo. There are many different species of indigenous plants and animals in the surrounding landscapes, which are composed of stunning volcanic structures and pine woods.

The Santiago Path:
Gran Canaria has its own Camino de Santiago, which crosses the island; this is not to be mistaken with the more well-known route in mainland Spain. This path travels through valleys, alpine areas, and coastal locations to provide a cross-section of the island's geography and ecosystems.

Park Tamadaba Natural:
Situated in the northwest, this park is well-known for its verdant pine forests—some of the island's finest preserved—that it boasts. There are routes for every skill level, from quick strolls to strenuous treks that, on clear days, reward

hikers with expansive vistas of the ocean and Mount Teide in Tenerife.

Guayadeque Barranco:
This ravine is a cultural gem in addition to a natural marvel. There are cave homes there that date back to pre-Hispanic times. The valley is home to several indigenous plant species, and its pathways go through a lush environment with traditional dwellings set into the rock.

The Natural Park of Pilancones:
This park, which lies in the south, stands apart from the neighboring popular beaches due to its rocky plateaus and steep ravines. The location is ideal for seeing migrating birds and preserves a large tract of pine woods in the Canary Islands.

Reserve of Inagua:
The preservation of the critically endangered Gran Canaria blue chaffinch depends on this biosphere reserve. Hiking in

this reserve entails taking cautious steps on trails that preserve the habitat of the birds while taking in the tranquility of one of the island's least impacted locations.

The Blues:
Los Azulejos, which is often visited as part of a trip around the Inagua Reserve, is renowned for its breathtaking greenish-blue rock formations that are the result of volcanic materials eroding. A little hike called "Azulejos de Veneguera" highlights these amazing natural wonders.

Preservation and Safety Advice

It's important to be ready and considerate while visiting Gran Canaria's natural areas:

Always wear sunscreen, bring extra water, and carry a map or GPS since not all routes are well marked.

Before starting a trek, check the weather since circumstances may change quickly at higher elevations.

To lessen your influence on the ecosystem and lower your chance of becoming lost, stick to designated paths.

Be mindful of the local flora and animals; avoid trampling on plants and don't disturb wildlife.

For more difficult routes, think about hiring a licensed local guide to improve your experience and guarantee safety.

Gran Canaria is a hiking and nature lover's dream come true with its astounding variety of natural beauty and well-maintained paths, providing an immersive journey into the heart of the Canary Islands' distinctive ecosystems.

B: Magnificent Terrain and Natural Structures

Gran Canaria is known for its remarkable diversity of landscapes and geological formations, earning it the moniker "miniature continent" often. This demonstrates the island's geological importance in addition to its scenic appeal. The following are some salient characteristics:

Roque Nublo:
Roque Nublo is a remarkable 80-meter-tall natural monolith that serves as a representative natural landmark for Gran Canaria. Situated more than 1,800 meters above sea level in the heart of the island, this ancient volcanic rock structure provides panoramic vistas and is the consequence of millions of years of volcanic activity.

Tejeda Caldera:

The Caldera de Tejeda, a sizable erosional basin or caldera centered on the towering Roque Nublo, provides evidence of Gran Canaria's volcanic beginnings. Following the cooling of the lava inside the volcano's vent, erosional processes created this enormous depression, which ultimately caused the volcano to collapse. Terraced slopes, craggy cliffs, and a variety of lush vegetation are some of its breathtaking views.

Caldera Bandama:
Situated at a depth of around 200 meters and a circumference of roughly 1 kilometer, the Bandama Caldera is among the island's more recent geological formations, dating back approximately 5,000 years. Nowadays, farmland and vineyards are located inside the caldera's basin, on the fertile volcanic soil.

The Maspalomas Dunes:
The Maspalomas Dunes are perhaps one of the most famous sceneries. These dynamic,

constantly evolving dunes are found in the southern part of the island. Because of the dunes' ecological significance, they have been declared as a protected nature reserve.

Cueva Pintada:
An ancient Canarian aboriginal settlement's archeological site is known as Cueva Pintada or the Painted Cave. Numerous pre-Hispanic murals can be seen within the cave, and the nearby archaeological park displays the remains of old Canarian buildings, which is evidence of the influence of humans on the island's topography.

Agaete Valley's Tufa Formations:
Rich foliage and unusual tufa formations—a kind of limestone created by the precipitation of carbonate minerals from water bodies with ambient temperatures—can be found in the verdant Agaete Valley. They help to establish the valley's reputation for having abundant

greenery and high-quality agricultural products, especially coffee.

The Blues:
Because of the hydrothermal modification of volcanic rocks, these vividly colored rock formations, which span from green to purple, are well-known for their vivid colors. The vivid coloration of the rocks, which provides an amazing perspective, is caused by the presence of minerals like iron and copper compounds.

The Little Ones:
Pico de las Nieves, the island's highest peak at about 2,000 meters above sea level, is an excellent place to see the diversity of Gran Canaria's landscapes, from the island's central highlands to the coastal plains.

Western Coastal Cliffs:
The western shore of Gran Canaria is home to striking cliffs that plunge sharply into the Atlantic Ocean. The sea's erosive might

sculpted these magnificent cliffs, which provide striking views, particularly after dusk.

Guayadeque Barranco:
Another illustration of Gran Canaria's breathtaking topography is this Barranco or ravine. This steep-sided valley, home to a diverse diversity of indigenous flora and fauna, terraced hills, and old cave dwellings, represents the natural and cultural history of the island.

awareness of Gran Canaria's natural history and biodiversity requires an awareness of its diverse geological formations. This unusual island's climate, geological past, and present-day topography all work together to produce its sceneries, making it an intriguing place to visit for visitors, geologists, and nature lovers alike.

5. INDULGING IN REGIONAL CULTURE

A: Food and Dining Occasions

Gran Canaria, a microcosm of many cultures and climates, has a thriving and varied gastronomic scene that matches its topography. A complex tapestry of tastes emerges when one immerses oneself in the local way of life via food and dining experiences.

Classic Recipes

Arrrugadas papas con mojo:
A mainstay, these "wrinkled potatoes" are served with a side of mojo, a sauce that comes in two flavors: mojo Verde, which is a green and herbaceous accompaniment, and

mojo Rojo, which is a red sauce with a hint of spice.

Vieja ropa:
Meaning "old clothes" in literal translation, this filling stew blends beef, chicken, garbanzos (chickpeas), and a variety of vegetables, symbolizing the island's blend of Spanish and Latin American influences.

Bienmesabe:
Based mostly on sugar, egg yolk, and almonds, bienmesabe is a confection that pays homage to Gran Canaria's Moorish history and is often seen in the pastry windows of Canarian cities.

Gofio:
A traditional Canarian grain flour, gofio is used in a variety of Canarian dishes, including kneaded balls served as a meal compliment, thickeners for soups and stews, and even desserts.

Fish

Gran Canaria's cuisine heavily relies on fresh seafood because of its closeness to the coast. Fresh fish is plentiful every day at restaurants and beach shacks. Keep an eye out for meals such as "caldo de Pescado" (fish soup), "fried moray eel", and "grilled limpets".

Cheeses

Gran Canaria's cheese is yet another delectable treat. **Queso de Flor**, a specialty flower cheese, is created with a blend of sheep and cow's milk and set thistle flower, giving it a distinct taste and texture.

Cocktail

Strong, unique wines with character, like those from the Monte Lentiscal region, are a result of the volcanic soil on the island. Wineries in the area provide tours and tastings where guests may learn about different varietals including Malvasía and Listán Negro.

Eating Occasions

The "Mercado del Puerto" in Las Palmas is a foodie's paradise, providing a relaxed and engaging eating experience as you taste regional cuisine from a variety of vendors.

Cenar bajo las estrellas:
A few rustic eateries provide outdoor or indoor dining under the stars, creating a romantic atmosphere for their delectable food.

Tapas:
A trip through Gran Canaria's cuisine wouldn't be complete without tapas. Small quantities of regional cuisine are served at barras (bars) across the island, making them ideal for food discovery.

Guachinches:
These improvised restaurants are set up in the houses of local farmers, serving home-cooked meals and providing a genuine taste of Canarian hospitality and food, often with an educational component about farming in the area.

Cultural Events and Festivals

Experience the island's gastronomic delights at festivals like Fiestas de San Juan and Saborea (Taste) Tejeda, where tradition and celebration blend into a delectable celebration of regional cuisine.

Tasting Gran Canaria's food is like tasting the island's history, geography, and spirit. It is recommended that visitors dine where the people dine, try out new tastes with abandon, and converse with the chefs about the origins of the island's distinctive cuisine, which is a monument to its diverse cultural heritage.

B: Cultural Events, Traditions, and Festivals

One of the Spanish Canary Islands, Gran Canaria is a haven for explorers and sun worshippers as well as a bustling hub for culture vultures, with an abundance of festivals, customs, and cultural events that vividly depict the island's rich past.

Events

In Gran Canaria, each municipality takes great pride in celebrating its particular festivities. Here are a few noteworthy ones:

Festival:
With parades, music, and dancing that showcase the island's passion for partying, Las Palmas de Gran Canaria has one of the biggest and most vibrant carnivals. The

celebrations conclude with the "Burial of the Sardine," which serves as their climax.

Ramadan Festival:
This event in Agaete, which culminates in a customary prayer for rain at the Church of Our Lady of the Snows, has participants marching with branches to the accompaniment of flutes and drums.

Nuestra Señora del Pino's Romería:
The Virgin of the Pine, the patron saint of Gran Canaria, is celebrated on Teror with pilgrims from all around the island. It is one of the most significant religious events.

Canarias Day:
The whole archipelago celebrates Canarian culture on May 30th, showcasing traditional costumes, music, and dancing along with delicacies like "mojo" and "papas arrugadas."

Customs

Gran Canaria's Afro-Hispanic origins, subsequent European colonialism, and indigenous history have had a significant impact on the island's customs.

Canarian wrestling (Lucha Canaria):
An indigenous sport in which competitors attempt to knock each other out inside a sand circle known as a "terror."

The Dance and Music:
Folk dances like the "isa" and "seguidillas" are popular, and traditional folk music has melodies performed on the "simple", an instrument resembling a ukelele.

Arts and Crafts:
Crafts reflecting the island's culture include woven baskets, pottery, and traditional clothing, which are often on exhibit during fiestas.

Events in Culture

Gran Canaria has a wide range of annual cultural events that highlight its artistic and intellectual diversity.

Stage of Opera:
An annual opera festival is held in the capital, Las Palmas de Gran Canaria, drawing enthusiasts from all over the world.

Festival International de Film:
A celebration of film, the Las Palmas de Gran Canaria International Film Festival brings together movies and filmmakers from different cultural backgrounds.

San Juan fiestas:
Las Palmas de Gran Canaria hosts a citywide celebration to welcome summer, complete with bonfires, fireworks, music, and a flurry of activity on the beaches.

WOMAD:

Since 1993, Las Palmas has hosted the World of Music, Arts, and Dance (WOMAD) festival, which features performances by performers from all over the world.

These celebrations, customs, and festivals only represent a small portion of Gran Canaria's vast cultural diversity. They are a reflection of the islanders' joyful sharing and celebration culture as well as their respect for their past. Welcomed into this colorful cultural tapestry, visitors discover that the island's beauty is found in its people and their rituals as much as in its breathtaking scenery.

6. OFF-THE-BEATEN-PATH ADVENTURES

A: Hidden Gems and Secret Spots

Beyond its sunny beaches and busy resorts, Gran Canaria is a treasure trove for those who are ready to go off the usual route. These are a few hidden locations that are certain to provide a genuine and remarkable experience.

Beach Güigüi

Güigüi Beach is tucked away on the island's west shore and can only be reached by boat or a strenuous climb through isolated ravines. The breathtaking cliffs, immaculate beaches, and often a beach to oneself make the effort to go here worthwhile.

Valerón's Cenobio

The Cenobio de Valerón, a vast network of more than 300 caverns that was once an indigenous granary, is located to the north of Gáldar. This seldom-visited archeological site provides intriguing insights into the pre-Hispanic people's way of life.

Cernícalos Barranco

The dry south is a world apart from this verdant gorge. Hiking trails go through a lush environment dotted with tiny waterfalls and laurel trees, which serve as a home for the elusive kestrel, colloquially referred to as "cernícalo."

The perspective of La Sorrueda

La Sorrueda, a remote location close to Santa Lucía de Tirajana, provides expansive vistas. This area has palm trees, a peaceful dam, and the remarkable Fortress of Ansite, a historical site including caverns that acted as the last stronghold for the Canarian natives during the Spanish invasion.

Guayedra Barranco

This balance is not on most travelers' itineraries near Agaete. Trekkers may make use of an old Royal Road that was formerly used for communication between the islands and a variety of indigenous vegetation.

The Blue Charco

Nestled among the craggy cliffs of Agaete lies the charming natural pool known as El Charco Azul. Part of the thrill is the route to this blue paradise, which involves a drop through farms of bananas.

Tasartico

The little town of Tasartico is located away from the busier tourist areas and has access to a quiet beach that is ideal for people looking for solitude. There are other interesting ancient ruins nearby, such as "Las Tumbas de Tasartico."

Roque Bentayga

Roque Bentayga is an isolated monolith with breathtaking views of the Gran Canaria region. It is also of archeological and spiritual value. It's a location close to Tejeda that many tourists miss, yet it provides a strong link to the island's history.

These locations are merely the tip of the iceberg in terms of what explorers might find in Gran Canaria. Off-the-beaten-path explorers will be well rewarded with the island's hidden treasures and secret sites if they approach the area with deliberate research, respect for nature, and curiosity.

B: Traveling to Less Well-Known Attractions

One of the jewels of the Canary Islands, Gran Canaria has a plethora of lesser-known attractions that promise special and private encounters. The island has a mix of undiscovered spots, charming communities, and scenery that whispers stories of the archipelago's heart beyond the well-traveled pathways.

Barranco de Guayadeque, or Guayadeque Ravine:
This verdant valley, which meanders across the southeast of the island, is a tribute to Gran Canaria's unspoiled beauty. Trekking into the ravine offers a unique look into the island's troglodytic past, with cave dwellings, a church, and even eateries carved into the rock faces.

Valerón's Cenobio:
This vast network of over 300 chambers hewn into the rocks is to the north of the island and is said to have served as a communal granary for the Guanches, an ancient Canarian people. For those who like history, its historical importance and expansive vistas make it a worthwhile visit.

Submarine Adventure in Puerto de Mogán:
Puerto de Mogán, sometimes referred to as "Little Venice," is a charming fishing community with a system of canals that run beside the sea. Explore the rich undersea environment distant from the usual diving sites by plunging below the surface in a submarine.

Galdar's Painted Cave (Cueva Pintada):
This museum and archeological park reveal the island's rich pre-Hispanic past. The cave gives a glimpse into the life of the native inhabitants and has murals on its walls.

Natural Park of Pilancones:
High-altitude landscapes with indigenous flora, animals, and pine woods may be found in the less-traveled Pilancones. The peacefulness of this place stands in stark contrast to the busy beach resorts.

Old Town Aguimes:
Aguimes's beautifully renovated old town has narrow cobblestone alleys, typical Canarian architecture, and a relaxed vibe that sets it apart from the island's tourist hotspots.

Northern Sardinia:
Sardina del Norte, a little fishing community, has a golden sand beach with clean seas that are good for snorkeling and a real local atmosphere, making it a great place to spend a beach day away from the throng.

Cernícalos Barranco:

Trek through this lush valley filled with lush flora and tumbling waterfalls. With its milder temperature, it's a paradise for endemic birding.

Tasartico Valley and Tasarte Beach:
Tasarte, which is reachable by a winding road, provides a secluded beach getaway, while the nearby Tasartico Valley offers breathtaking scenery and hiking paths.

The Cave District and Artenara:
Nestled among lush greenery and scattered with cave dwellings, Artenara is the island's most scenic town, perched atop a mountain range.

These lesser-known sights give visitors a closer look at the island's natural splendor and reveal the richness of its culture. Undiscovered corners of Gran Canaria provide peaceful escapes from the popular resorts, beckoning the daring visitor to discover the island's diverse allure.

7. USEFUL ADVICE AND HINTS

A: Lodging Selections and Suggestions

Gran Canaria offers a wide range of lodging choices to suit every taste:

Hotels:
Options abound on the beaches and in the interior, ranging from luxurious resorts to inexpensive hostels. Popular destinations include Maspalomas for a more sedate, affluent experience and Playa del Inglés for nightlife. If you're looking for luxury, check out the Lopesan Costa Meloneras Resort or Maspalomas' Seaside Palm Beach. Travelers on a tight budget may choose lodging in Las Palmas, such as Hotel Pujol, which provides value without compromising location.

Vacation Rentals and Apartments:
Located throughout the island, particularly in popular areas, these rentals are perfect for those looking for self-catering accommodations. Numerous options are listed on websites like Airbnb and Vrbo, ranging from studio apartments on the beach to rustic homes in the highlands.

Rural Tourism & Agrotourism:
Intimate accommodations are available in fincas and country homes (casas rurales). A glimpse of the island's lush interior splendor may be seen at locations like the Hotel Rural Las Tirajanas and Finca Molino de Agua near Fataga.

Camping & Caravanning:
For the more daring visitor, there are a small number of expanding campsites. There are basic to well-serviced facilities, some of which are situated in or close to natural areas.

Recommendations for Lodging in Gran Canaria

Make reservations early:
Space is limited, especially during the busiest times of the year.

Location matters:
Choose between the hustle and bustle of a destination like Las Palmas de Gran Canaria and the more sedate, scenic communities that are located inland.Considerider transit**: If you're not renting a vehicle, it can be more practical to stay near bus lines or in walking neighborhoods.

Read reviews:
First-hand accounts in reviews may provide valuable insight into smaller lodgings such as B&Bs or flats.

Off-season steals:

Visiting at off-peak times might result in fewer crowded attractions and more affordable rates.

Look for package discounts:
Occasionally, booking lodging and travel combined might result in substantial savings.

Authentic stays:
For Canarian hospitality, take into account casas rurales.

Always verify amenities:
Make sure your lodging has Wi-Fi, air conditioning, or any other services you may need.

Travelers may choose lodging that enhances their experience of Gran Canaria's distinct character and varied scenery by keeping these pointers in mind.

B: Going About the Island and Getting Around

There are many ways to learn about Gran Canaria that may be customized to fit various tastes and travel plans. This is a comprehensive guide on island transportation:

Rent a Car:
One of the most well-liked ways to see Gran Canaria is by renting a vehicle, which gives you the flexibility to go to secret locations, mountain towns, and secluded beaches. There are rental companies near the airport, in larger cities, and in popular tourist destinations. Although most roads are kept up well, be ready for narrow roads in the highlands.

Guagua Buses:

The firm 'Global' operates a vast public bus network in Gran Canaria. Locally referred to as "guaguas," the buses link Las Palmas, the airport, and other resorts, and they travel the majority of the island. In rural regions, buses are less frequent but dependable and reasonably priced.

Busses Las Palmas City:
There is a different bus service called "Guaguas Municipales" that runs inside the capital, Las Palmas. Popular locations including Playa de Las Canteras and the ancient Vegueta are frequented by these buses.

Taxis:
If you don't want to wait for a bus or shorter excursions, taxis are a practical choice. Taxis may be located at taxi ranks, called in advance, or hailed on the street in crowded places. For larger parties, the metered fares are more affordable.

Biking:
Cycling around the island is a beautiful experience. Bike rental establishments may be found, particularly in popular tourist regions. This is better suited for more experienced riders due to some difficult terrain, especially in the inner mountains.

Trekking and Strolling:
Walking may be enjoyable for short distances, particularly in cities or resorts like Puerto de Mogán, Puerto Rico, and Playa del Inglés. Gran Canaria is a great place for hikers, with an extensive network of routes for the more daring among you.

Grapes:
There are ferry services from Puerto de Las Palmas and Agaete to the adjacent islands. They provide an attractive means of visiting Tenerife, Fuerteventura, and other islands.

Motorbikes and Scooters:

They are available for hire and provide a comparable amount of freedom as vehicles, but they also make parking and navigating through traffic simpler.

Tour Buses:
Las Palmas offers hop-on, hop-off tourist buses that provide commentary and a comprehensive overview of the city's attractions.

Take into account the following for each option

Verify Schedules:
Bus and ferry schedules are subject to change, particularly on weekends and holidays.

Driving:
Make sure you have a current, valid driver's license that is accepted in Spain before hiring a car.

Route Planning:
Having a thorough map might be helpful since GPS devices may not work well in certain isolated or hilly locations.

Transport Cards:
To get cheaper bus prices, think about obtaining a transport card such as the "Tarjeta Insular de Transporte" (TIT).

Making effective use of various modes of transportation will enable you to fully appreciate Gran Canaria's range of landscapes and cultural offers.

8. INSIDER INSIGHTS AND RECOMMENDATIONS

A: Insider Tips for a Memorable Stay

If you want to have an unforgettable experience away from the masses while visiting Gran Canaria, take into consideration these insider tips:

Remain in a country Casa or Finca:
Rather than booking a typical hotel room, go for a country home or finca, especially if you're staying in the interior of the island, such as Tejeda or Artenara. This gives you a more genuine experience and gives you a connection to the local way of life.

Dine with Locals:
Look for possibilities to have dinner with a local family rather than going out to eat.

Utilize services that link visitors with nearby hosts to enjoy authentic home-cooked meals.

Early Morning Hikes:
Hike early in the morning on trails like Barranco de los Cernícalos or Tamadaba to avoid the heat and congestion. These routes provide the most tranquil sunrises.

Visit Local Markets:
Look for regional goods in Las Palmas' Mercado de Vegueta. If you want fewer crowds and wider choices, it's better to arrive early.

Acquire Some Spanish Phrases:
Although most people in tourist regions speak English, you may improve your interactions with locals by learning a few Spanish words. It's an act of respect for the way of life there.

Take Part in a Fiesta or Romeria:

If you happen to be visiting during a time of celebration in the area, take part. You'll get a personal look into Canarian dance, music, and culture.

Travel to the North:
Places like Agaete are still seldom visited. See the natural ponds at Las Salinas or the Dedo de Dios rock formation.

The Island's Secrets Revealed to an Adventurous Explorer

Roque Nublo's Less-Traveled Paths: There are lesser-traveled paths offering seclusion and breathtaking views in addition to the main road. Find out about these hidden paths from a local guide.

Cueva de los Candiles:
Seldom seen by visitors, this cave has pre-Hispanic cave art. It's not well publicized, so you'll probably require an experienced guide.

Hidden Beaches:
Maspalomas is well-known, but you should also check out Guayedra Beach near Agaete or Playa de Güi Güi, which are only reachable by boat or a strenuous climb and provide isolated beauty.

Important Cultural Activities Off the Tourist Trail

Lucha Canaria (Canarian Wrestling):
Take in a local bout of this age-old sport. It provides a unique cultural spectacle and is held in local communities in sand circles.

Local classes:
In communities like Santa Brigida, take part in classes for traditional crafts like pottery or basket weaving. A portion of the island is yours to make and take home.

Authentic Cuisine:

Go out to eat in the mountain villages. Seek for restaurants that serve regional dishes like "vieja" (parrotfish), "papas arrugadas" with "mojo" sauces, and "ropa vieja," a stew of chickpeas and beef.

Vineyard Tours:
Canarian wines have a unique flavor due to the volcanic soils. Take a tour of the Bandama region vineyards to sample wines and see how they are made.

Music and Dance:
Learn about traditional folk music and dance by going to events or gatherings where musicians play songs with a "simple" accompaniment and people dance "is" and "folías."

Using these tips to enhance your trip to Gran Canaria will undoubtedly make it more memorable and give you tales to tell long after your trip is over. To maintain sustainable tourism practices, always approach such excursions with respect for the environment and local culture.

B: Undiscovered Treasures and Must-See Attractions

Must Visit Locations

Maspalomas Dunes:
The dunes provide a distinctive scenery on the island, akin to a tiny version of the Sahara. It's highly suggested to take a camel ride during sunset.

Roque Nublo:
Another famous emblem of Gran Canaria is this old volcanic rock. Trekking to the top offers breathtaking views.

Cenobio de Valeron:

This archaeological site, a maze of old granaries, provides a window into the island's pre-Spanish past.

Teror:
A major religious center with vibrant marketplaces, it is renowned for its stunning basilica and typical Canarian architecture.

Casa de Colón:
This museum explores the history of the Canary Islands and its relationship to Christopher Columbus. It is situated in Las Palmas.

Poema del Mar Aquarium:
A more recent addition to Las Palmas, this aquarium has striking exhibits of marine life from all around the globe.

Undiscovered Treasures

Barranco de Guayadeque:

A lush gully including eateries and cave homes. It provides an opportunity to take in the island's scenic splendor away from the throng.

Tamadaba Natural Park:
This park is ideal for anyone looking for peace due to its secluded beaches and verdant pine trees.

Puerto de Mogán:
This fishing community, often called "Little Venice," has quaint alleys and winding canals despite its lack of widespread recognition.

Barranco de Los Cernícalos:
An ever-flowing creek forms an uncommon, verdant terrain that is home to laurisilva, a Tertiary-era forest type.

Güi Güi Beach:

Only reachable by boat or a strenuous climb, this remote beach provides peace and unspoiled surroundings.

Arucas:
The massive neo-Gothic cathedral and the Arehucas Rum Distillery, which provides tours and tastings, are the two main attractions of the old town of Arucas.

Aspects Culturally

Local Cuisine:
This includes items like "ropa vieja" and "papas arrugadas" with "mojo" sauce.

Traditions:
Canarian wrestling, traditional music, and the "isa" dance.

Fiestas:
The lively culture of the island is shown by regional celebrations like "Carnaval" and "Fiesta de la Rama".

Local Workshops:
Look for workshops where craftspeople make traditional products like knives and ceramics if you're looking for genuine mementos.

Wineries in the Bandama Caldera:
Local vineyards may provide delicious and educational experiences. Canarian wines are a hidden delight.

Secret Advice

To avoid crowds, visit at off-peak hours.
Talk to locals to find out about secret locations and less-touristy places to eat.

Take public transportation to explore lesser-known sites slowly.
Seek out regional marketplaces to purchase one-of-a-kind handicrafts.

A variety of attractions, from natural beauties to historical sites, can be found on Gran Canaria, with many hidden gems just waiting for the more daring visitor to find them.

9. ADDITIONAL INFORMATION AND RESOURCES

A: Helpful Links and Websites

Gran Canaria's Official Tourism Website: www.grancanaria.com
This is the Gran Canaria Tourist Board's official website. It's a key source of information for visitors looking for details about the island, including lodging, things to do, and upcoming events.

www.grancanarianaturalandactive.com is the website for Gran Canaria Natural and Active:
This website offers comprehensive information on hiking routes, rural tourism, and natural reserves on the island for

individuals who like the great outdoors and the natural world.

Tourist Information Centers (CITs):
All across the island, several tourist information centers assist with maps, guides, and personal suggestions. Important hubs are located at the Gran Canaria Airport, Playa del Inglés, and Las Palmas de Gran Canaria.

Global Bus Services:
www.globalsu.net
The bus system on the island is run by GLOBAL and provides a convenient means of transportation. Timetables, route data, and fare information are all available on the website.

The Cultural Agenda of Cabildo de Gran Canaria may be found at www.grancanariacultura.com.

The cultural agenda of the island government contains details regarding performances, exhibits, music, and the arts.

Accessibility to Gran Canaria:
www.predif.org
A website that offers information about services and accessible tourism for visitors with particular requirements.

Fred. Olsen Express:
Maritime Transport: www.fredolsen.es/en
Fred. Olsen Express offers ferries for island hopping trips and mainland transportation. Online booking options and schedules are offered.

Trails for Hiking

Gran   Canaria:
www.wikiloc.com/trails/hiking/spain/canar
y-islands

A list of well-documented hiking trails that includes user-uploaded photos, elevation, and length.

Medical Assistance in Gran Canaria:
Emergency: 112
This is the general emergency number that will put you in contact with emergency medical, fire, and security services right away.

Information about the Gran Canaria Airport:
www.aena.es/en/gran-canaria.html
Access to airport services, real-time flight information, and links to other transportation.

Consulates and Embassy:
If not on Gran Canaria itself, the majority of nations maintain consulates or embassies on neighboring islands. Visit the website of your government to get precise contact details.

Festivals and Cultural Events:
www.hellocanaryislands.com
An extra source of information on area news, weather, and events in the Canary Islands.

Environmental and Safety Awareness:
www.112canarias.com
Information on environmental protection guidelines and safety requirements is essential for every tourist who wants to enjoy the island in an environmentally conscious manner.

Resident and Expat Resources:
https://grancanariainfo.com
A wealth of knowledge for foreign nationals and extended guests, including tips for living and working on Gran Canaria.

These sites provide a wide range of information that is very helpful when organizing a vacation to Gran Canaria. They guarantee a well-planned and engaging vacation by providing a strong basis for comprehending the island's services, cultural offers, and infrastructure.

B: Additional Reading and Planning Materials

When organizing a complex trip to Gran Canaria, having trustworthy sources for in-depth analysis and up-to-date information is essential. A selection of recommended reading and planning materials is provided below.

Sources and Handbooks:
1. Insight Guides' "Gran Canaria" provides much cultural and useful information.
2. Rambling Roger's "Walk This Way Gran Canaria" focuses on hiking routes and walking pathways.

3. Sunflower Books' "Gran Canaria Car Tours and Walks" is a great resource for nature hikes and self-guided excursions.

Websites and Blogs Online:
1. The official tourist website for the Canary Islands, [Hello Canary Islands](https://www.hellocanaryislands.com), offers a wealth of information.
2. [Expert on Gran Canaria](https://www.grancanariaexpert.com) A local's advice and guidance to secret locations.
3. Trails and exploring the natural world are the focus of [Hiking in Gran Canaria](http://www.walkinggranCanaria.com)

Communities and Forums for Travel:
1. The Gran Canaria Forum on TripAdvisor offers Q&A and the latest traveler reviews.
2. Lonely Planet's Thorn Tree forum: Travel professionals respond to questions about destinations.

3. Expat Exchange: Great for helpful tips on living and housing.

Movement:
1. Global SU [Official Site] (https://www.globalsu.net)
Information on the island's bus service, including routes, times, and costs.
2. Compare rental car prices with [CICAR](https://www.cicar.com) and [AutoReisen](https://www.autoreisen.es).

Events in Culture:
1. Gran Canaria Cultural Calendar: Up-to-date festival and event schedules.
2. WOMAD Las Palmas - Details of the annual international music festival (https://www.womad.org)

Maps and Navigation:
1. For offline navigation, use applications like Maps. me and Google Maps.

2. Get a thorough road map of Gran Canaria so you can navigate while you're on the move.

Local tourist Offices:
1. For brochures and tailored suggestions, stop by Gran Canaria's local tourist offices. On occasion, they may provide discounts and vouchers for nearby events and attractions.

Room:
1. [Booking. com](https://www.booking.com)
Extensive selection of lodging options, including studios and hotels.
2. Check out [Airbnb](https://www.airbnb.com)
For additional experiences living in the area.

Food and Restaurants:
1. Reserve tables and find restaurant specials using

[ElTenedor](https://www.eltenedor.es) or [Atrápalo](https://www.atrapalo.com).
2. You may get a taste of what to anticipate by following food bloggers and Instagram accounts that feature island cuisine.

Teaching Languages:
1. To learn simple Spanish phrases, use applications like Duolingo or Babbel.
2. When traveling in remote areas, an excellent compact Spanish-English dictionary may be very helpful.

In terms of health and safety, Europeans traveling inside the EU should have the European Health Insurance Card (EHIC).
2. To find out whether any immunizations are advised, contact your local health authority.

You may create a comprehensive trip to Gran Canaria by combining these resources, which will guarantee a satisfying mix of leisure, culture, and discovery.

10. CONCLUSION - EMBRACING THE WONDERS OF GRAN CANARIA

A jewel among the Canary Islands, Gran Canaria presents a microcosm of divergent landscapes, from the green ravines of the north to the undulating dunes of Maspalomas. This is an island that wants to be fully experienced—it is not something to pass by.

In conclusion, exploring Gran Canaria's diverse array of cultures, landscapes, and experiences is essential to fully appreciating its beauty. It's about realizing how the island can be both a playground for adventurers and a safe sanctuary for rest.

Gran Canaria's different climatic zones, which create micro-environments that protect a wide variety of flora and animals, attract tourists. Understanding the island's distinct ecosystems is essential to appreciating its appeal. Large routes for hikers and nature lovers may be found in the pine-clad mountains and laurel woods, while seaside towns provide vibrant places to attend vibrantly colored local celebrations.

On the island, eating is a celebration, and the variety of the local cuisine is reflected in it. Tasty seafood, fruit from the tropics, and hearty cheeses showcase the regional products and make for a palate-pleasing meal. Enjoy this side of Gran Canaria by savoring regional specialties such as "papas arrugadas" with "mojo" sauces.

The story of Gran Canaria's beaches is told in its chapter. Every beach has a story to tell, from the quiet Amadores to the busy Las Canteras. To completely embrace them, to spend time in the sun, to hear fishermen's stories, to play in the waves of the Atlantic.

The inhabitants of the island are its heartbeat. Talk to the people there; they are proud of their history and can tell you what the real essence of the island is all about. Their customs, music, and tales are contagious and will never be forgotten.

We must travel responsibly to protect the island's natural beauty for future generations. To express thanks for the pleasure Gran Canaria offers, one may minimize ecological impacts, honor animals, and support local companies.

Ultimately, the key to fully accepting Gran Canaria is the readiness to recognize and honor its unique personality. It's a sun-filled haven of adventure, comfort, and warmth. It's a place that reminds us of the amazing variety of the planet in addition to being a place to retreat.

In summary, Gran Canaria should not be quickly crossed off a list of places to visit. For those who are eager to discover its marvels, it's a world within an island that keeps on opening up. Carry its memories with you on your next adventure, and embrace it wholeheartedly, curiously, and with an open heart.

Here are some well-planned tours in Gran Canaria for various interests:

Tour Highlights: Three Days

First Day: North and Las Palmas

- Morning: Begin your tour of Vegueta, Las Palmas' historic area. See the Canarian Museum and Casa de Colón.

- In the afternoon, walk along Las Canteras Beach after seeing Tafira's Jardín Botánico Canario.

- Evening: Savor regional seafood at a restaurant by the seaside on the promenade.

Central Gran Canaria, Day 2

- In the morning, make your way to Teror, a charming village. Take a look at the Nuestra Señora del Pino Basilica.

- Afternoon: See Roque Nublo in the highlands after exploring the Caldera de Bandama's natural surroundings.

- Dinner in the evening: Tejeda is renowned for its almond pastries.

Day 3: The Dunes and the South

- In the morning, stroll or ride a camel in the Maspalomas Dunes.

- In the afternoon, unwind at the more sedate Playa de Mogán or Playa de Amadores.

- Evening: Take advantage of the Yumbo Centrum's nightlife or treat yourself to a spa treatment at one of the hotels.

Seven-Day Island Discovery

Days 1 through 3: Begin with the 3-Day Highlights Tour.

West Coast Adventures on Day 4

- Proceed to the charming fishing resort of Puerto de Mogán by way of the picturesque west coast.

- If you're feeling adventurous, make a stop at Playa de Güi Güi, or go to Los Azulejos for amazing pictures.

Northern Wonders on Day 5

- Swim in Agaete's natural swimming pools. - See the Painted Cave of Galdar and the Cenobio de Valerón.

Day 6: Land-Based Investigation

- Investigate historical locations such as Cueva Pintada or pay a visit to Fataga located in the Valley of the Thousand Palms.

- Take in San Bartolomé de Tirajana's rustic attractions and regional handicrafts.

Day 7: Culture and Recreation

- Spend a day relaxing; consider going swimming or golfing.

- Go to museums, such as the Atlantic Center of Modern Art or the Elder Museum of Science and Technology.

10-Day Immersion (To Get Off the Beaten Path)

Days 1–7: Adhere to the 7-Day Island Exploration schedule.

Mountain Villages on Day 8

- Explore the culturally vibrant villages in the central highlands, such as Artenara; and stroll along the historic Caminos Reales, which connect the towns.

Day 9: Hidden Aways in the Northeast

- Explore the less-traveled northeast, including stops to view the massive Gothic church at Arucas. Savor a tranquil day on Quintanilla's beaches or Tafira's Las Palmas neighborhood.

Day 10: Living Locally

- Explore the local way of life by going to a market, like the Mercado de Vegueta. In the Triana neighborhood, savor tapas and the lively street life on a nighttime stroll.

Keep in mind

Every day should be scheduled with individual interests, travel schedules, and opening hours in mind. Travel time may be reduced by making reservations for lodging throughout the island. Because renting a vehicle gives so much freedom, it's typically the most convenient method to move about. For up-to-date information about attractions, always consult your local resources as times and circumstances might vary.

Printed in Great Britain
by Amazon